Scooter mania

Jeremy Case

Illustrated by Zac Sandler

PENGUIN BOOKS

Thanks to Dr Philip Bell and Jill Pollock, both of Musculoskeletal Medicine –
BUPA Wellness; Kate Hodges; Andrew Diprose and Jamie Hooper.
Dedicated to Shiroma De Silva.

Please note that anyone attempting the tricks in this book does so at their own risk and should use appropriate safety equipment.

PENGUIN BOOKS

Published by the Penguin Group
Penguin Books Ltd, 27 Wrights Lane, London W8 5TZ, England
Penguin Putnam Inc., 375 Hudson Street, New York, New York 10014, USA
Penguin Books Australia Ltd, Ringwood, Victoria, Australia
Penguin Books Canada Ltd, 10 Alcorn Avenue, Toronto, Ontario, Canada M4V 3B2
Penguin Books India (P) Ltd, 11 Community Centre, Panchsheel Park,
New Delhi – 110 017, India
Penguin Books (NZ) Ltd, Cnr Rosedale and Airborne Roads, Albany,
Auckland, New Zealand
Penguin Books (South Africa) (Pty) Ltd, 5 Watkins Street, Denver Ext 4,
Johannesburg 2094, South Africa

On the World Wide Web at: www.penguin.com

Penguin Books Ltd, Registered Offices: Harmondsworth, Middlesex, England

First published 2000
1

Text copyright © Jeremy Case, 2000
Illustrations copyright © Zac Sandler, 2000
All rights reserved

The moral right of the author and artist has been asserted

Designed by Dan Newman/Perfect Bound

Made and printed in England by Clays Ltd, St Ives plc

British Library Cataloguing in Publication Data
A CIP catalogue record for this book is available from the British Library

ISBN 0–141–31155–X

Contents

We Have Kick-off!

When the shiny, sleek, lightweight Micro Skate scooter arrived in the UK in October 1999, many people wrote it off as just another craze. Newspapers and magazines described it as 'another Furby' and 'the new yo-yo', thinking that the fad would pass as soon as the gleam on the aluminium wore off. How wrong they were.

> **'It's the most fun I've had not on a surfboard.'**
> *Simon, 28, Micro*

Updated for the millennium, the scooter has taken the globe by storm. Kids are using them for fun, adults are riding them to work, and their popularity shows no sign of fading. At present, they're selling at a rate of 300,000 a week worldwide.

The appeal of the scooter – apart from its hugely stylish design – is that it's as light as a laptop, can be folded up quickly, and fits into a backpack. You can carry it with you wherever you go – down the park, on the tube or even to a fancy restaurant. It's ideal for short journeys of can't-be-bothered-to-walk length.

Unlike bikes, there's no problem with security as you don't have to lock them up to a dodgy drainpipe. Unlike skateboards, you're much less likely to fall off. And unlike rollerblades, you don't have to waste time sitting around putting them on and taking them off. The scooter's ready to roll in two ticks and three clicks.

Scooters are ideal for this environmentally aware, exercise-obsessed, time-is-money age. People are using them instead of driving or jumping on a bus, and they're getting a workout at the same time. It's exercise without the hassle. On the flat, you can scoot about as fast as you can run (but with far less go-go juice), and on hills you can glide down with the minimum of effort. When you get to the bottom, if you don't fancy pushing up the other side, you can just pick up your machine and walk.

As if they weren't cool enough already, scooters have been given an added dose of kudos by a whole A-list of celebrities. In London, Robbie Williams and Kylie Minogue have both been seen surfing the asphalt on their Micros, while in New York, Oscar-winner Kevin Spacey rode his electric scooter on to the set of David Letterman's talk show and declared it the only way to get around.

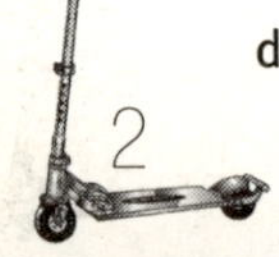

In cities, parents are doing the school run on them. In Bristol, Asda-WalMart has issued staff with scooters to help them get round the huge shop floors. Executives use them to bank through the city traffic to meetings. And mums and dads who've bought them for their kids soon find they're 'borrowing' the scooters themselves to nip down the shop for a pint of milk.

On university campuses, the Micro name has become as famous as Nike and Microsoft. At motor racing circuits such as Silverstone and Brands Hatch, pit crews use motorized Go-Peds for running errands. In Helsinki airport, luggage porters zip around on specially customized models built to carry heavy suitcases.

In the US, internet companies stage races across warehouse-style offices, Micros being the essential piece of equipment for any self-respecting dotcom entrepreneur. In film studios, staff use them to get between sets. Even former skateboarders have been converted and are now using them to do tricks. And in parks the world over, kids ride them, well, simply because they're brilliant fun.

super models

From the local park to Finnish marathons, from scooters you can buy in the high street to ones you can only dream about – they're all here. Remember, it takes all types.

PUSH POWER – get a kick out of these!

THE MICRO SKATE SCOOTER

Known as the Razor outside Europe, this stylish machine was the first push scooter to arrive on the modern scene and launched a whole chasing pack of copycats. The Swiss-designed, Chinese-produced Micro is still the most popular, thanks to its patented folding mechanism, durability – the heat treatment on the aluminium makes it stronger – and for its natty, get-around-town cool.

The slightly more pricey Micro Pro comes with front suspension (to reduce the 'judder'), funky clear-blue wheels, LED (Light Emitting Diode) back lights that flash when you hit a jolt (yep, they're on most of the time) and a 'wheelie bar' at the back, for the stunt people among you.

If you liked this you'll like: The new Micros – the Air and Air Flex (see p 82).
Web site: www.citybug.co.uk/micro.html

'I like it because it becomes little.'
Enrique, 12, Micro

THE JD BUG

Leading contender from the huge army of Micro imitators, mainly because it was actually brought out by the same company. More gimmicky than the original, and with a crazy slogan: 'Step on, bug out', it comes in five colourways – orange, blue, red, green and black – and you can mix and match the wheels, grip tape, straps and handlebars. Otherwise it's almost identical to the Micro, except with an extra inch on the footplate, which now finishes alongside the rear axle to give the back end of the scooter a bit more oomph. Even cheaper is the Micro Fun, which is exactly that.

If you liked this you'll like: The Viza Kikit (see p 68).

Web site: www.jandrsports.co.uk/index-2.html

'Our house has three and all my friends are getting them. Wow! We just love them, especially the new bright colours.'
Alexandra, 12

THE KNOW-PED

Californian petrol-scooter-experts Go-Ped's only foot-powered machine is more old-skool and less hi-tech than the Micros, like a step back in time to the hippy sixties. The wider board and extra front brake, along with a wheel mechanism that just screams out for BMX-style stunt pegs, all mean that the Ped's not only more suitable for longer trips than the Micro, but it's just peachy for performing tricks. Especially in those colours – Flaming Yellow, Ferarri Red and Beach Boy Blue. A real good-time scooter.

If you liked this you'll like: The antique one you'll find in your parents' loft. **Web sites: www.goped.com/Home.htm www.landsurfing.com/pushped.html**

> **SPECS**
> - aircraft-quality high-carbon steel foldable frame
> - front caliper and rear wheel spoon fender brake
> - 150 mm non-pneumatic natural rubber wheels
> - weight: 5.45 kg

THE K2 KICKBOARD

The only scooter that should be ridden sideways, the three-wheeled Kickboard is designed for the PlayStation generation, with a joystick for steering. Just push it left or right, lean the bend-tastic board and the two front wheels will track round to where you want to go. Hopefully. Plus, the bend in the board gives you a far smoother ride. This cross between a skateboard and a scooter costs a few bucks more, but it's by far the coolest machine on the market, a serious West Coast skaters' piece of equipment for surfing the urban landscape, built for trendsetters who've never grown out of their boarding sneakers. Customize with either Downhill tyres, for Formula One speed freaks, or Offroad wheels, for cross-country rally drivers (see page 53).

> **SPECS**
> - injection-moulded aluminium foldable frame
> - springy wood/fibreglass deck
> - three 100 mm polyurethane smoke wheels
> - rear wheel guard brake
> - weight: 3.2 kg

If you liked this you'll like: The K2 Carveboard, a four-wheeled, sloping-decked monster (see p 82).

Web site: www.kickboard.de

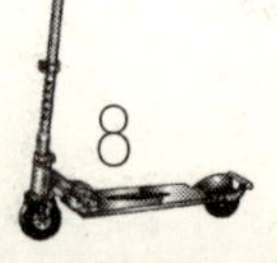

PETROL POWER – for 'big kids' only

THE SPORT GO-PED

If you're the lazy type who likes to feel the wind in your hair, this is the baby for you. Find a bit of wasteland and you'll be burning rubber – with a few modifications, you can even get the speed up to over thirty miles per hour. (If you think you're really cruising, why not enter the world championship races they hold in California?) The Sport boasts several 'world records', including 'the greatest power-to-weight ratio of any transportation device in the world'. But all you need to know is that it's the ultimate toy for today's urban warrior. The convertible sports car of the scooter world.

SPECS
- 22.5 cc engine
- max speed: 20 mph
- range: 25–30 miles
- foldable frame
- front caliper and rear wheel guard brakes
- 150 mm non-pneumatic natural rubber wheels
- weight: 9 kg

If you liked this you'll like: The Hoverboard, Go-Ped's first electric model, the scooter that feels like you're really hovering.
Web site: www.goped.com/Home.htm

ELECTRIC POWER – charge up, charge off

THE CITYBUG

The scooter for grown-ups, the sleek Citybug's advantage over your basic moped is its weight and foldability, plus the fact that you can recharge it from any old plug socket. 'It's designed for short, exhilarating trips into work,' says spokesman Steve Malkin. 'You can drive it through the office right up to your desk if the boss isn't watching.' The Bug boasts a seat, proper brakes and, bizarrely, teeny pedals on the front wheel, which are only just larger than your big toe. However, the only exercise you're likely to get is building up your biceps lugging it around.

SPECS
- 150-watt motor, battery life one hour, rechargable in five
- max speed: 15 mph
- range: 12 miles
- bicycle lamps
- 500 mm pneumatic wheels
- weight: 21kg

If you liked this you'll like:

A Vespa. Or the surely imminent Sinclair C5 revival.

Web site: www.citybug.co.uk

PLAIN WEIRD – scooters from outer space

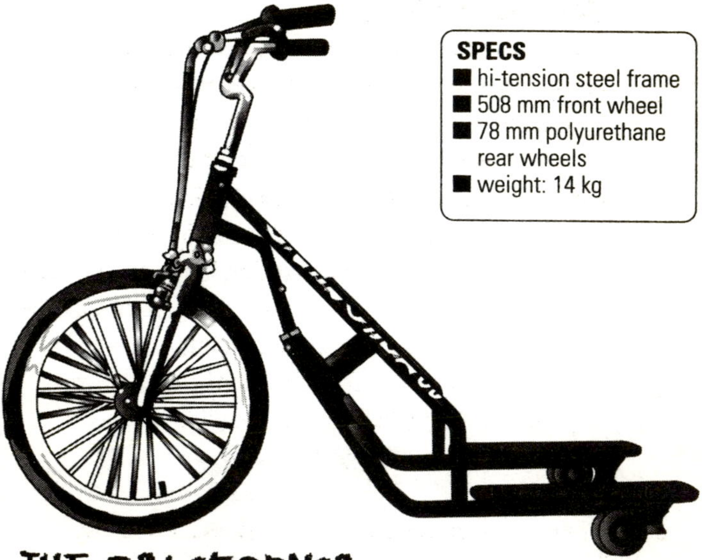

SPECS
- hi-tension steel frame
- 508 mm front wheel
- 78 mm polyurethane rear wheels
- weight: 14 kg

THE CALIFORNIA GRAND CHARIOT

It looks like the result of a nasty accident between a BMX and a couple of skateboards, and brings back memories of that tricycle you used to have when you were three, but one thing's for sure – if you scooted down the high street on this, you'd certainly turn a few heads. In fact, you'd probably put a few people's necks out. Comes in black and blue, which is the colour you'll be if you keep getting confused about what it is exactly that you're riding. Only the Americans could have come up with this hangover from the Roman Empire. But if you've seen *Ben Hur* and reckon yourself as a bit of a gladiator, this is the only way to get around this AD.

If you liked this you'll like: Sorry, we just can't work you guys out.
Web site: www.californiachariot.com/GC.html

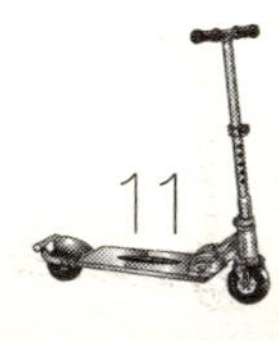

THE KICKBIKE SPORT CLASSIC

Straight out of Finland, this half-bike was created in the early nineties by medical student and world kicksled champion Hannu Vierikko so he could train over the summer. Now kickbiking itself has gathered momentum and become an international sport in its own right, especially in Germany, Finland, USA, Czech Republic and Holland, where they hold regular events, including marathons. To prove what his contraption could do, or maybe just to show off, Vierikko himself rode 437 miles across the Rockies in 1998 in a week, reaching speeds of 60 mph downhill. But no longer is it just seen as a

training tool for endurance athletes – it's recently become popular with couriers in Europe, is big on US college campuses and has just hit the streets of New York. It's cheaper than a bike and costs less to replace if stolen, has few moving parts to maintain and no greasy gears so you won't get your shoelaces stuck in the chain, plus dismounting is easier than falling off a log. It may look like something your grandad used to wobble around on, but 12,000 fans worldwide can't be wrong.

If you liked this you'll like:

The Dirtsurfer – not technically a scooter as it has no handlebars, but a wicked piece of kit nonetheless, like a thin metal longboard with BMX wheels (www.ep-x.com/dirtsurfer).
Web site: www.kickbike.com

SPECS
- steel frame
- standard road bike front wheel
- 457 mm rear wheel
- high-pressure puncture-resistant tyres
- bicycle brakes
- weight: 9 kg

'The Kickbike is a gas. It's a lot of fun to play with.'
Tom, 36, Kickbike

Other makes cluttering up shop shelves

Foot-powered

* Blade Runner, Bulldog, California Chariot, E Shock, Exit Street Scooter, HCF-501 Foot Mini Scooter, Kick Inline Scooter, Mini Scooter Rollerboard, Mi3, 900R TT, Quickstep Mini Scooter, Racer, Razor Rollerboard Scooter, Rock Voxa, Rollerway, Skoooch, Stickboard, Tamitalos Fashion Scooter, Twister, Viza Kikit, Xootr Comp, Xootr Cruz, Xootr Street

petrol-powered

* BigFoot, Blata Blatino Buzz Board, Go-Quad, Liquimatic, Swift, X-Ped, Viza Cruze, Viza Venom and Viza Viper (both with optional snow attachments, including a front ski and solid studded rear wheel!)

Electric-powered

* EMX Racer, EMX Custom Model, Four-wheel Electric Leisure Scooter, Hoverboard, Two-wheel Electric Leisure Scooter, Zappy Electric-Powered Scooter, Zappy Mobility, Zip Electric Scooter

CELEBRITY RIDERS

The rich and famous are abandoning their chauffeur-driven limousines in favour of a healthier way of pottering around between photo shoots and recording studios. Here are just some of the sightings ...

on push scooters

* Robbie Williams, Kylie Minogue, Prince Harry, Harrison Ford, Patsy Palmer, Gail Porter, Keith Flint from the Prodigy, Ewan McGregor, Jack Dee, Richard Branson, Sarah Jessica Parker, Jonathan Ross, Reef, Lolly, Sadie Frost, Jude Law, Kirk Douglas, Angela Rippon, Jean-Paul Gaultier, Chris Eubank, Creed, and Norman Wisdom

on motorized scooters

* Boyzone, Jennifer Love Hewitt, Melanie Sykes, Kevin Spacey, Sharleen Spiteri from Texas, Finley Quaye and Noel Edmonds

Spin Doctor

Like rollerblading and skateboarding, scooting is a top laugh. But even on those tiny wheels you can zip around at a right old speed, so you need to take care and, like Ali G, show some respect for all the people around you. Follow these guidelines and you'll soon be scooting like a real pro.

* Wear the same safety gear as you would on a bike. A helmet and knee and elbow pads will protect you if you go for a tumble, especially if you're trying new tricks.

* **Make sure the handlebars are at the right height, and use them for steering, not leaning on, lazybones. One jolt and you'll be straight over the top. You should stand up straight, with your weight on the back wheel – that way it's easier to steer too. If you're bending over all the time, you'll end up walking around like a gibbon when you're older.**

* Use your scooter in parks and wide open spaces. Busy areas are no fun in any case because you'll have to keep stopping all the time. Anywhere with plenty of room and a smooth surface is ideal. If you have to, scoot on the pavement, but *never* on the road.

* **Push off first time on a flat, crack-free area. Your scooter will tackle bumps with ease once you've got some speed up, but you may go flying if there's no momentum. If you're on the pavement, aim for the middle of the slabs so you don't spin out in the cracks.**

* When you're scooting, it's easy to end up staring at your feet all the time. Don't fall into this trap – make sure you look up and around for any looming obstacles or innocent pedestrians minding their own business.

* **Watch yourself in the rain. Brakes become less efficient and are liable to slip.**

* Keep your foot on the brake when you're going downhill or round a curve. You never know what's round that corner.

HOT TIPS

* Swap your legs over as soon as one starts getting tired. If you always use the same foot to push with you'll end up with one thigh three times bigger than the other and your trousers won't fit you any more.

* **Don't use the skateboarding/surfing stance and do the sideways thang. Stand with your foot pointed forward and in the centre of the deck for stability and balance. Not only is it bad for you to twist your body, but it looks pants too.**

* You've heard of tennis elbow, well now there's a new condition called **scootists' shin**. When you get off your scooter and pick it up, be very careful. The little fellas' bases will often spin round and give you a nasty whack on the shins. And bruised legs are *so* not a cool look.

✪ **Wear a rucksack to carry your clobber and to put your scooter in when you're not using it.**

✱ If you've got a mobile phone, don't answer it while you're on the move. You'll fall off and embarrass yourself.

CARE

✪ **Keep a beady eye out for bald patches on the back wheel if you do a lot of tricks. The brake wears down the plastic and you won't be able to stop so well. If you use your scooter regularly, the wheels will probably have to be replaced every three months. But that's OK, because you can get some funky new ones in different colours (see p 53 – ACCESSORIES).**

✱ Keep the moving parts well oiled, especially if you've been out in the wet.

✪ **Polish it regularly to maintain that straight-outta-the-box gleam.**

✱ It's not just your scooter that needs looking after. If you're always forgetting to swap pushing feet, you'll wear down one of the soles on your shoes much quicker than the other, and unless you buy a new pair of trainers every three months, you'll end up walking round with a bizarre kind of limp.

People who would be a bit wobbly on a scooter

- **Kenny** from *South Park* (in fact, anyone from *South Park*, seeing as they don't have any legs)
- **Godzilla** (not sure he could fit his foot on the board)
- **David Ginola** (he'd do himself an injury with all that diving)
- **Long John Silver** (obviously)
- **Joey** from *Dawson's Creek* (all that emotional baggage wouldn't be good for balance)
- Any of the **Teletubbies** (they're not exactly streamlined, are they?)
- **Tiger Woods** (he'd be straight down that pothole in one)

People who would be ace on a scooter

- **David Beckham** (best right foot in the business™)
- **Harry Potter** (he'd love a spell on a scooter)
- **Tony Blair** (to get down with the 'youth')
- **Prince William** (to get round the endless marble-covered corridors of Buckingham Palace. And he could borrow his little bruv's)
- **Stuart Little** (although he might have to lower the handlebars)
- **Bart Simpson** (obviously)
- **Buzz Lightyear** (because he can go to infinity and beyond)

TRICKS OF THE TRADE

All you need is a scooter, safety gear, loads of space and a crowd of admirers. If it takes you a while to get the hang of these stunts, don't worry. Skateboarders spend most of their time falling off and everyone still thinks they're cool.

Make sure you read the Spin Doctor's safety tips (p 16) before you start!

Any self-respecting scootist should have these tricks up their sleeve.

THE MANUAL

Your good old-fashioned wheelie, called a Manual on a scooter because you have no pedals. Either while moving or standing still, put your weight at the rear of the scooter and lift up the front wheel using the handlebars.

Difficulty rating: ✶

THE CROUCH

Lower the handlebars as far as they'll go, give yourself a run up and then get down on your haunches. Turn your body slightly sideways to squeeze both feet on to the scooter and bingo! Low-bridge hassles are a thing of the past.

Difficulty rating: ✳✳

THE BONUS

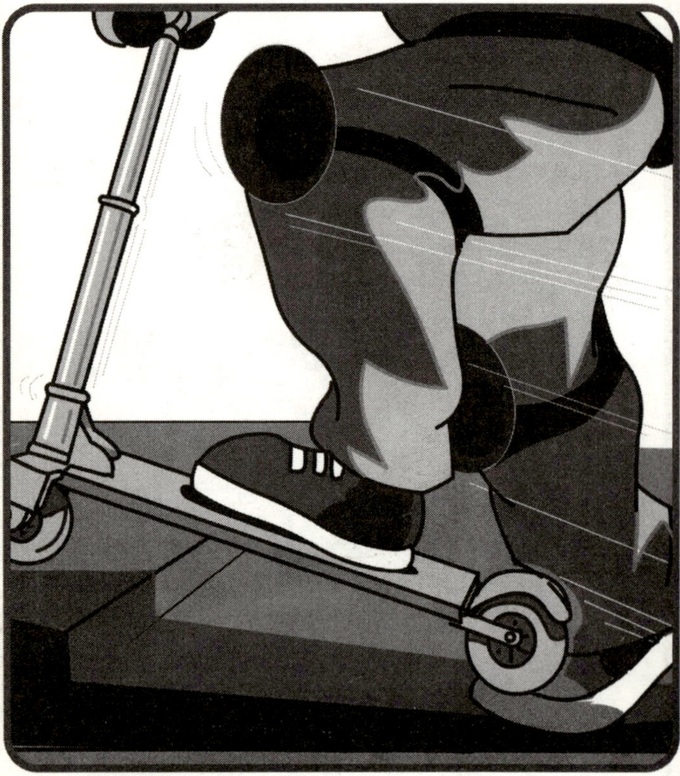

Perfect for negotiating a step up without even breaking your stride. Just before reaching it, push down on the ground with your foot, lift up the handlebars and you're off and away.

Difficulty rating: ✶✶

THE TWO-WHEELER

Exclusive to the generously a-tyred Kickboard, this one.
Stand on one side and lean in the opposite direction.
Lift one of the front wheels off the ground and make
like a pavement James Bond. Not to be attempted in a
narrow alleyway as you'll veer off into the wall.

Difficulty rating: ✳✳✳

THE HANDS-OFF

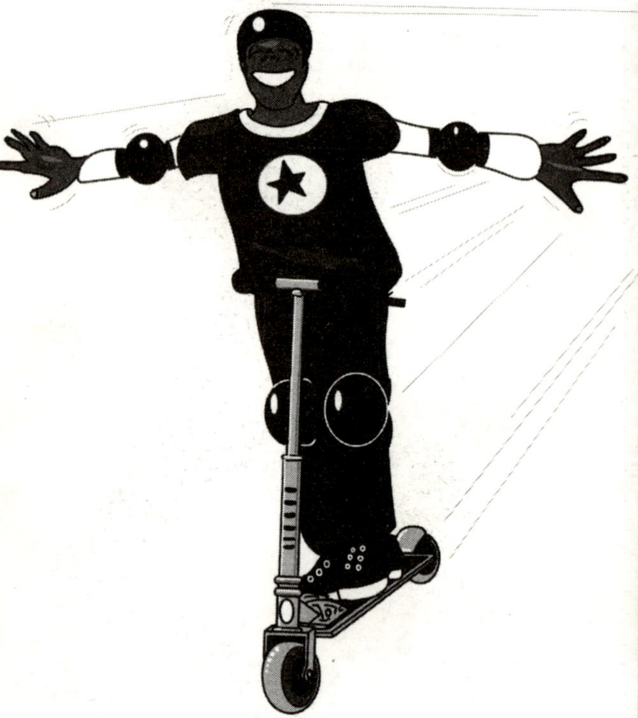

Get up a head of speed, lean against the handlebar with your body and just let go. Practice by taking one hand off at a time until you've cracked it. You're the king of the world!

Difficulty rating: ✖✖✖

THE FEET-OFF

You'll need better balancing skills than a performing sea lion, but it can be done. Build up some pace, tuck the handlebar into your midriff and lift yourself up, sticking your legs out either side of the T. Don't try to combine it with the Hands-off, though.

Difficulty rating: ✹✹✹✹

THE OLLIE

1

Skateboard classic invented by fourteen-year-old Alan 'Ollie' Gelfand, a whopping twenty-two years ago. Basically a jump while moving. Bend your knees and push down on the scooter (easier if you're on a springy Kickboard) to propel yourself up in the air. Requires a bit of mastering – poor old Ollie used to get his shoes and boards stolen by jealous skaters who thought he was using glue to stick his feet down.

Difficulty rating: ****

2
3

THE ENDO

A reverse Manual, when you lift the back wheel off the ground. Much easier on a Know-Ped thanks to the front brake, but still possible on a Micro if you stand towards the front, jump slightly so there's no weight on the scooter and push the handlebars forward at the same time. Don't push too hard though, or your face will become best friends with Mr Tarmac.

Difficulty rating: ✹✹✹✹✹

Keep this up and you'll qualify for the scooting Olympics.

More of a skatepark trick, because it's easier if you launch yourself off a ramp. When you're airborne, grab hold of the board with one hand and stick the opposite leg out. It can be done on the flat, mid-Ollie, but you'll need niftier feet than Michael Owen.

Difficulty rating: ✳✳✳✳✳✳

THE GRIND

Another old skateboard favourite. Ollie up on to a step and then slide along it for as long as you can hold your balance, before peeling off and back into your stride. Don't worry, you're not cheating if you use your foot to push yourself back down – this is hard enough with four wheels, let alone two.

Difficulty rating: ✳✳✳✳✳✳

2
3

THE BUNNY HOP

They used to say BMX boys have a lot of fun, but now it's the revenge of the scootist. Do a Manual and with one foot on the rear brake, play keepy-ups like Ronaldo's scooting cousin, bouncing up and down on the back wheel. If you're a bit tasty, you can either swap feet mid-jump, bounce round in a circle (known as a Brake Pivot) or spin the handlebars. Do all three at once and you're a scooting legend.

Difficulty rating: ✳✳✳✳✳✳✳

THE HANDLEBAR REVERSE

You thought handlebars were just for turning? Fool. If you're bombing along fast enough, you'll be able to flick them round so fast (so that the grip in your left hand is now in your right) that you'll still keep going in a straight line. Don't try it on a Know-ped though – you'll get all tangled up in the front brake cable and end up on the floor with those 'tweet tweet' things circling above your head. Like in cartoons.

Difficulty rating: ✱✱✱✱✱✱✱

THE CHERRY PICKER

1

From the BMX stable. Standing still, put one foot round the stem and back on to the scooter so you're facing the wrong way with the handlebars in front of you. Swap your hands over and then move the same foot round again to return to where you started.

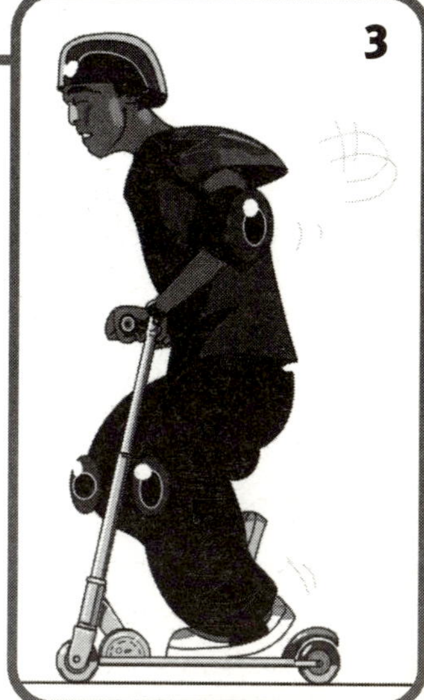

If you've got a Know-Ped,
attach stunt pegs to the
front wheel to stand on like
a true BMXer. Like going for
a spin without even moving.

Difficulty rating:
✳✳✳✳✳✳✳

NEAR-IMPOSSIBLE

If you can do these, pack your bags and join the circus.

THE 180

1

2

Start with a jump up, Ollie-style, then spin through half a circle and land going backwards. What you do after that is anybody's guess. Probably safer to just slow down until you stop, if you haven't fallen off already.

Difficulty rating:
✱✱✱✱✱✱✱✱

THE 180-DEGREE REVERT

1

2

With your foot on the back brake, do the 180, but land
as if you're doing a wheelie. Use your momentum to
swivel round through another 180 degrees, bringing the
front back down when you've completed the circle.
Don't practise too long though – you'll end up dizzier
than when you put your forehead on a broom handle
and run round it twenty times.

Difficulty rating: ✖✖✖✖✖✖✖✖✖

THE TAIL WHIP

1

Do an Ollie and simultaneously kick the rear of the scooter out with your back foot. It should spin round once beneath you like a helicopter blade until you land back on it. Until you perfect this high priest of the scooter stunt kingdom, practise by taking a step halfway through, lifting your foot up as the scooter boomerangs back. Advisable to wear shin pads for the first 428 attempts.

Difficulty rating: ✗✗✗✗✗✗✗✗✗✗

ME AND MY BABY

Three scooter fanatics tell us why their model is the best thing since the invention of the wheel.

WILLS AND HIS MICRO

I've got two Micros and one Know-Ped. I got my first Micro from Club Blue Room in London in March 2000. I went down to Brighton seafront to get the hang of it and I've been riding it ever since. They're absolutely brilliant, so lightweight and dynamic. And when I'm not using it, I just fold it up and carry it over my shoulder.

I used to walk everywhere, but now I prefer the Micro. The Know-Ped is quite a lot bulkier and heavier, but that's still portable and comfortable to ride as well. Scooting's a brilliant sport and it does cut time. It used to take me ten minutes to walk from my door to the tube, now I can do it in three.

I'm a host at the Millennium Dome so I ride it around for work from zone to zone because the Dome is so big. I spend about two hours a day on it. It can wear your leg out, but I don't really notice as I'm used to walking. Sometimes I swap feet.

People think it's just a kids' thing – they remember having scooters when they were younger – but now it's for adults as well. These Micros, they're the urban soul's scooter, personal transport for the new millennium. You've got to be careful where you go, you can feel the roughness, but I think I've mastered most surfaces.

I've been down quite a few hills in Somerset, but you've got to be very careful because the wheels are quite small. I'm still working the tricks out. The only one I can do at the moment is to lift myself up and stick my feet forward. I've only fallen off once, but they are pretty easy to come off.

I got the extra scooters for my friends, so that we can all go out together. I went to Paris last weekend with a friend and took the two Micros.

People stared and asked questions – but you can buy them over there as well. They're a huge craze all over the world at the moment. I'm going on holiday to Italy next month so I'm going to take both scooters again. I might get a really bright yellow or orange one so that it really stands out.

Wills Gardner, 36, tourist guide at the Millennium Dome

JOE AND HIS K2 KICKBOARD

My Kickboard's lasted me over a year now. I hate walking, that's why I bought it. I got it in August 1999 from Snow & Rock in Kensington and I was the fifth person in London with one. Everyone was like, 'What is that? Did you make it?' It's a pretty cool little device, still works well.

I bought it to go travelling with. My mate told me that Australia was really good for skating cos it's really smooth and flat – and it was such a saviour, I was just razzing around everywhere. When I arrived, Micros had already caught on, but no one had seen a Kickboard before and they were amazed. Everyone that had a go on it said that it was totally better. It was a good talking point as well; good for impressing the ladies.

The Kickboard's quite low to the floor so when you're pushing, you don't even have to bend your leg. That's why it's so much better than a skateboard – you can just cruise. It's a luxury way of travelling, but on those little Micros, it's hard even to get two feet on it.

In Bali I took it along the beach and people would give me a tow on their mopeds. I met quite a few people just by having it. And it was excellent at airports because I had a suitcase with wheels. Airports are the best location – the floor's like marble, it's just saying, 'Skate me.'

Now I use my scooter to get to work. It's the best get-around thing. It takes about twenty minutes off my journey. It gives me more get-up-and-go in the mornings because I know that it won't be too traumatic getting to work. And I just laugh at all the people stuck in cars.

A bike is faster, a skateboard does more tricks, but the beauty of the scooter is that it folds up. On the scooter, you're much more in control and it's so quiet and smooth people don't even hear you coming. The thing is, pedestrians don't walk in straight lines, especially when they've just woken up and they're going to work. So I'd put a little horn on it, a little 'meep meep', as I've run into the back of people when they've changed direction right in front of me.

I have hurt myself once. I tried to jump off a bandstand and I landed it, but I took the weight on my knees and bent down and the joystick caught me in the ribs and that really hurt, but it didn't do any lasting damage.

I reckon to do really good tricks on it, to compete with the skateboard, they would need to change the design slightly because it's not very easy to pull off the ground. I can jump up a high step, but nothing higher than that really. But my little matey here, Pod, he can jump on it and he's only six.

If I designed my own one, I'd put more bounce in it – maybe suspension in the front forks, so that you could push your weight down and jump up. If there was spring in the handle it would reduce the feeling of arthritis in your hands too because it does vibrate a lot. And I'd change the grip. I reckon it should be a handle so that you could actually pull it up and get some serious air.

I'm planning to buy one of the new ones. The wheels are a lot bigger so you'd be starting to compete with bikes and it looks like it could do some serious concrete-burning. Very nice construction. But with this one, I've got my £200-worth, definitely.

Joe Plimmer, 24, photographer

ALICE AND HER SPORT GO-PED

I used to have a BMX when I was a kid and loved it. Then I tried my boyfriend's Go-Ped and I was addicted straightaway. It takes a couple of goes to get used to, but you get the hang of it quite quickly. And it's so much fun.

I bought my own one in May 1999 through a friend who's got a car garage in Lincolnshire. Second-hand, you can pick them up for around £200. We go to Beetle Bashes quite a lot and they sell them there, or at festivals like V2000. Mine's dark blue, but I want to spray it all pink and sparkly.

At weekends we go to the skatepark in Peterborough or this really big deserted car park, which is good because it's got kerbs that you can jump up on to and skid along. There's a whole group of us – four with Go-Peds, a couple with Monkey Bikes, like miniature motorbikes, and some on BMXs.

I can do jumps, wheelies and this trick where you put your stomach on the handlebars and stick your arms and legs out so you're in a star shape and carry on cruising. I'm trying to do a 180, but I keep stalling. I've seen people jumping over others lying down. You wouldn't catch me doing the

lying down though! Loads of people I know have had accidents, just scrapes and bruises really. But I don't like to risk it. I'm not as daredevil as they are.

I've bought extra suspension and an air filter for it, a big chrome thing, which makes the Go-Ped last longer and increases your speed, but I really got it because it's good for hooking your foot under so it's easier to do tricks. I've also got an underboard that fits beneath the scooter so you don't break it in two. And I wear a helmet. Mine's an Evel Knievel skaters' one.

> **'I'm just on my way to meet a friend in my lunch hour. If I didn't have my scooter I probably wouldn't bother because it's too far to walk.'**
>
> *Sally, 23, Micro*

We've taken them with us on holiday a few times. That's the handy thing about the Go-Ped, you can pick it up and take it everywhere. In Whitstable it was excellent because there was a really, really long path all the way along the beach, so we just bombed it up and down there.

I think Micros are boring. You may as well walk. I like to go fast, to get somewhere quickly. I can get up to twenty-five miles per hour on my Go-Ped and if I need exercise, I'll go to the gym. It's not heavy to carry around either, there's only a tiny engine. Actually, usually I just leave the motor running and walk along with it. It's very lazy, I know, but then that's why I got a scooter in the first place.

My dad has a go on it, and he's fifty-three. All the old blokes absolutely love it. They're like, 'Can we have a go?' It's just a big boy's toy. I reckon I'll still be pottering around on it when I'm a pensioner too, but by then everyone'll be floating about on hover scooters.

Alice Davies, 24, picture researcher

Scooter Fashion No-nos

What you *won't* be wearing this season!

* **Motorcycle crash helmet** complete with visor (We're surprised you got up the courage to leave the house.)

* **Bellbottoms/flares** (Like having a couple of sails on your legs. You'll never get any speed up.)

* **Leg in plaster** (Hobble home and eat some grapes.)

* **Studded football boots** (You may be late for training, but you'll be straight into the treatment room if you emergency stop.)

* **Wellies** (That's not what we meant by burning rubber.)

* **Umbrella** (Leave it to Inspector Gadget.)

* **High heels** (You'll take someone's eye out.)

* **Cape/shawl** (You're not Batman you know. And if the wind whips it up into your face you'll be in trouble.)

* **Tight skirt** (Especially if you're a boy.)

* **Backpackers' rucksack** (You'll be so top heavy, you'll be pulling permanent wheelies.)

CHANGING VROOMS

With so many scooters now on the streets, stand out from the pack by giving yours a makeover and adding some individual touches. Personalize your scooter by mix-and-matching accessories or do a spot of DIY to make it truly one of a kind. Then, when you've finished, why not give it a name? Go on, you know you want to.

ACCESSORIES
Stuff you can buy down the high street

MICRO

Replacement wheels come in various colours such as red, green and blue. Or act like a Formula One star and make a pit stop when it rains with a spare set of black wet-weather wheels by Bridgestone. Even funkier are light wheels, which are transparent with red, white and blue flashing LEDs. Get your inlines online at **www.micro-mobility.com**.

Rubber handlebar grips again come in different colours, from black, yellow and red to transparent blue. Naturally, all are recyclable, as you'd expect from such an environmentally friendly product.

Other add-ons include a wheelie bar, which fits on the back and helps with tricks, knee-friendly suspension, coloured shoulder straps and motion-activated LED 'brake' lights that simply slot into the two triangular holes at the back of the board. Carry everything round in your black nylon Micro bag, which folds up into a pouch to strap on your belt when you're on the move. And look out for a new Micro clothing line, coming soon for all you fashion heads.

GO-PED

Find cool designer decks at **www.abentone.fsnet.co.uk/ABENTWEB/Page_7x.html** . Bad boys should try the Evil, while speed freaks will be attracted to the Clear, which is transparent so you can see the ground rush past underneath you.

KICKBOARD

Swap your treads for some extra-wide Downhill slick tyres for extra speed or pneumatic rubber Offroad wheels to give those bumps short shrift. You can even buy locks, bags and, for sucker-like grip, special trainers with an Air Heel and Boarder Sole.

CUSTOMIZING

The only limit here is your own imagination. In Japan, where there are entire magazines devoted to scooters, you'll never see the same machine twice. 'A Japanese cowboy came in once, she was like Tonto,' says Ashley Larkman from skate shop Club Blue Room in London. 'She had a huge cowboy hat, a shirt with all the tassles, cowboy boots with spurs and her scooter had all these fluffy mascots and lights on the handlebars. She had a finger bell on it too and you could hear her coming down the street, "Ding ding, ding ding". We'd be like, "Here she comes again."'

Don't let them have all the fun – get in on the act with these top tips.

GRIP TAPE

Not only does it look cool, but it'll help you with tricks because when you stick it on to your board, it'll give you extra ... er ... grip. The plain black variety looks a bit like sandpaper and comes in rolls, which you can then cut up as you please to make your own patterns. Or buy special logo strips – there are thousands of skate-type designs, so there's something for everyone. Check out any skate shop.

STICKERS

Bung 'em on anywhere except the wheels, where they'll come off in the wet. Scour toy shops for your favourite characters from the telly or big screen, or try the Internet. Sites such as **www.stickemup.com** have cool skateboardy designs and retro fireball stickers from the 1970s, which can be ordered online from the States. Even better, if you're a bit of a computer whizz, you can create your own styles on a PC – maybe try writing your own name in a funky design – and then take the disc into any signwriting shop, tell them what colours and materials you want and a few hours later you'll get your eager hands on your very own personalized sticker.

STOMP PADS

Little metal or plastic devices that snowboarders use for grip when they climb off the ski lift and back on to the board. You can just as easily stick them on to your scooter, either to help with tricks or just to make it look cool. They come in all shapes and designs, are about ten centimetres wide, and can be bought from snowboard and outdoor-pursuity shops.

ANODIZING

For seriously cool customizers only. Anodizing is a complex scientific process that you might remember from chemistry lessons. But all you need to know is that it permanently changes the colour of the metal on your scooter, unlike paint, which can chip off. Just take your scooter into any metal-working joint and tell them what you want. You can dye the whole scooter – make it gold, brass, sparkly blue, whatever – or take it apart and just do a few nuts and bolts. Either way, you'll be the envy of all your mates.

Scooting Stars

Find out whether you were born to ride with these special horoscopes.

Aries – The Ram
21 March–20 April

Adventurous and full of energy, the ram is the first to get in on any craze, the scooter being no exception. You're a real daredevil and love big challenges. Energetic Arieans will try anything once, including the most complicated tricks – hey, who cares about sore cheeks when you're having fun?

Top tip: Stay safe and wear protective gear.

Taurus – The Bull
21 April–21 May

You were born to ride and are never happier than when scooting through your local park among the luvverly trees and flowers. Scooting is right up your garden path because it doesn't harm the environment. Practical and down-to-earth, you prefer straightforward scooting from A to B rather than showing off with fancy footwork. Don't just plough through those potholes though – remember to go round them.

Top tip: Take the bull by the horns. Be adventurous and try something new.

Gemini – The Twins
22 May–21 June

You're quite restless and can easily lose your concentration. As a result you find it difficult to master new moves and tend to give up if it doesn't come easy first time. This may have something to do with the two sides of your personality battling with each other. At least you shouldn't have any problems remembering to swap your feet over.

Top tip: Keep at it – practice makes perfect.

Cancer – The Crab
22 June–22 July

You're an emotional type and can be very sensitive. If anyone should make a snidey remark about your scooting style, like the crab, you will retreat into your shell and sulk for days. But when you're in a better mood, people find you kind and caring, and always the first to help other scootermaniacs.

Top tip: Remember to go forward, not just sideways.

Leo – The Lion
23 July–23 August

You're the king of the urban jungle. Like the lion himself, you love being the leader of the pack and you'll usually be found scooting along at the front of your friends. You tend to be the one who decides where to go and what to do and your mates naturally follow you. You've also got a big heart and will be first to the scene to help if someone goes for a burton.

Top tip: Don't get too bossy with your posse!

Virgo – The Maiden
24 August–22 September

You're a complete perfectionist who spends hours making sure your scooter retains that box-fresh appearance. You keep it so clean you can see your Puma Sprints' reflection in the board. You wouldn't be seen dead without all the right gear and you practise all your moves in private – no one is allowed to watch you until you're 100 per cent accurate.

Top tip: Relax and don't be afraid to make mistakes.

Libra – The Scales
23 September–23 October

If scooter rage breaks out, you'll usually find a Libran trying to sort out the argument fairly. Librans have a very strong sense of justice and love peace and harmony in their lives. They also love beauty and are attracted to the sleekest, most expensive scooters. Should have no problems with balance either.

Top tip: Looks aren't everything, so forget appearances and focus on fun.

Scorpio – The Scorpion
24 October–22 November

You're prone to jealousy and may find yourself eyeing up other people's scooters, especially if they've got the latest Micro Double Air Flextastic Super-Pro. Possessions are very important to you and you get attached to special things very easily. Once you've got yourself a shiny new scooter, you won't let it out of your sight.

Top tip: Let your mates have a go occasionally.

Sagittarius – The Archer
23 November–21 December

You love a challenge and if you're a typical Sag you can be found trying things like 720-degree double backflips – tricks no one else has ever heard of, let alone attempted. You love to lark around and don't take yourself too seriously – which is just as well, as you're always falling off in public places. Doh!

Top tip: Look where you're going.

Capricorn – The Goat
22 December–20 January

You're a sensible mountain biker who's been slowly filling up the piggy bank for months, saving for the scooter of your dreams. Once you've got it in your sweaty little hands, you'll spend all your spare time perfecting your basic technique before going anywhere near an 'Ollie', or whatever it is those other kids call them. You're a stickler for getting things right.

Top tip: Throw caution to the wind and try some of the tricks in this book – you might actually enjoy them!

Aquarius – The Water Carrier
21 January–18 February

Bright, bold Aquarians love new ideas and you were probably one of the first people in your area to get a scooter. Independent and strong-willed, you prefer to go out scooting on your own rather than with a group, worried that you'll end up looking like something out of the Red Hand Gang.

Top tip: Try being more sociable. And avoid those puddles, water-lover. You'll come a cropper.

Pisces – The Fishes
19 February–20 March

Dreamy Pisceans are usually off with the fishes and enjoy scooting around at their own pace, just going with the flow in their own little world. The Pisces sign rules the feet and as a result you are capable of some pretty nifty little moves – you should be a dab hand at the tail whip in particular – so long as you can put your mind to it.

Top tip: Stay alert and snap out of your daydream, otherwise you'll go straight into the back of that pedestrian.

Snippets of sidewalk sour grapes

- ✳ 'What time's your mum expecting you back for tea?'
- ✳ 'Get off the pavement.'
- ✳ 'It's hop-along Cassidy.'
- ✳ 'Show us a trick.'
- ✳ 'Can I have a backie?'
- ✳ 'Watch out for the lamp pos ... Oh, too late.'
- ✳ 'Any slower and you'll be going backwards.'
- ✳ 'What's your other scooter, a Porsche?'
- ✳ 'Just get the bus like everyone else.'
- ✳ 'Aaaaaaaaaaaaargh!'

The inventor

'I created the scooter because I was too lazy to walk to my favourite sausage place.'

Micro inventor Wim Ouboter is well on his way to becoming a millionaire – just from being lazy. The forty-year-old former Swiss banker designed his first scooter in 1994 because he couldn't be bothered to walk twenty minutes to get a takeaway. Now the craze has spiralled so much that he's talking about it becoming an Olympic sport.

'I created the scooter because I was too lazy to walk to my favourite sausage place, the Star Grill,' he admits. 'It was one of these awkward distances and I thought there had to be something that you could take out of your closet, put under your arm and off you go.'

So he set about building a contraption that would ease the rumbles in his stomach. Over the next two weekends he built his first prototype scooter, using inline skate wheels and an old bike column. But things didn't go quite according to plan. 'It worked, but people were laughing at me in the street,' he says. 'Everyone thought I was crazy – even some of my closest friends.'

Disappointed, Wim abandoned the scooter in his garage for three years and forgot about it. But fortunately for us, the local kids didn't. 'While I was at work, the children from my neighbourhood saw the scooter and would ask my wife if they could have a ride. Sometimes there were sixteen kids waiting for their turn. My wife said, "There's something about this scooter, you need to take it seriously."'

So, he went back to the drawing board, put some more of his own money in, and came up with a more lightweight and stylish model – the Micro. After numerous failed attempts to get financing, he finally found a manufacturer in Taiwan prepared to gamble on

> **'I can do jumps and wheelies. I fell over once and hurt my knee, but it's not difficult. You just get on them and scoot around.'**
> *Jack, 10, Micro*

his machine. Today, his Taiwanese partner employs 6,000 people in three factories in China, churning out 50,000 Micros per day.

Wim had always known that scooters were fun – he'd been riding one since he was five. His parents had bought him and his two sisters scooters because one sister was born with one leg shorter than the other and couldn't ride a bike. But he had no idea how popular they would become.

'I was not expecting so many people from five to seventy to be using scooters,' says Wim, who these days zips around on the Kickboard and the new Micro Air Flex. 'But they're very easy to use – inline skates are a little more complicated and riding a bike is not as much fun.'

Now all his critics are laughing on the other side of their faces, and many of them are trying to copy his idea. Of the 100,000 scooters sold in Hong Kong in recent months, around seventy per cent were fake. 'They're even copying our name,' moans Wim. 'But my father said once, "If you get copied it's a compliment, because you've got a good product."'

'If pavements are too bumpy it feels a bit like holding a pneumatic drill, but on smooth surfaces you can get it up to a good speed, at least as fast as an average run. I fell off once when I was going down a hill too quickly. But apart from that I've had no real accidents.'

Polly, 26, Micro

Proud to be doing his bit for Switzerland, Wim still runs his worldwide scooter empire with just five staff from a two-bedroom apartment in Zurich. 'Hopefully we're getting away from our image of just making chocolate, watches, and Swiss army knives,' he says. 'Scooters are not a fad. This is just the beginning of the century of Micro mobility. It's not a joke any more. People really believe in the future of the scooter.'

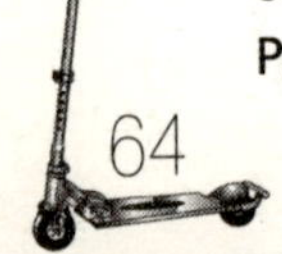

places NOT to go on a scooter

- **The Tour de France** (King of the Mountains? We think not.)

- **An expedition to Everest** (It'd be great for getting down again, but there's snow way you'd make it to the top!)

- **The countryside** (Especially anywhere with cattle grids – or cow pats ...)

- **An army parade ground** (Left, left, left, right ... aaargh! Saluting could cause a few problems too.)

- **The Sahara desert** (You won't be able to get much momentum up.)

- **A car wash** (Even more so if you're ticklish.)

- **The supermarket** (Do you really think those eggs are going to make it back in one piece?)

- **Bungee jumping** (Somehow we don't think you'd be able to stay on the scooter.)

- **The Eiffel Tower** (Too many steps. And they're all full of holes.)

- **A tightrope** (C'mon, you're not *that* good.)

The whizz-kid

'I built my first web site when I was ten and bought my first stocks and shares a year later.'

Most of us see a scooter and think fun: Dominic McVey thinks business. While other kids his age are out in the park, racing each other and doing stunts, fifteen-year-old Dominic is locked up at home in his bedroom on his computer, running his own internet business. He brings scooters over to Europe from America, earning more money than he could ever possibly fit in his pocket.

Scooter Boy, as he's affectionately known in the papers, runs the company Scooter UK Ltd, which ships motorized and push scooters over the Atlantic, and it's made him into Europe's youngest self-made millionaire.

'I built my first web site when I was ten and bought my first stocks and shares a year later,' says Dominic. He then began importing gadgets like minidiscs, MP3 players and portable hi-fis from Japan that you couldn't buy in the UK for family friends, as well as organizing end-of-term parties at school, selling tickets for five pounds a pop.

> *It's just convenience for me. It takes me ten minutes to get to work, compared with half an hour by tube.*
> **Fumihito, 27, Micro**

Together with birthday and Christmas money, he managed to raise £3,000 to set up his scooter business. When he sent an e-mail to Viza Motors asking to be their UK distributor, he didn't mention he was only fourteen. 'I didn't think it was necessary,' he says. 'I thought scooters were ideal for everyone in Britain as traffic problems were getting so bad and I knew I could do a good job. I wouldn't say I foresaw the scooter craze, but I was determined to set one in effect.'

Now his weekly turnover is heading towards a staggering £15 million as he deals with fourteen countries throughout Europe and his web site

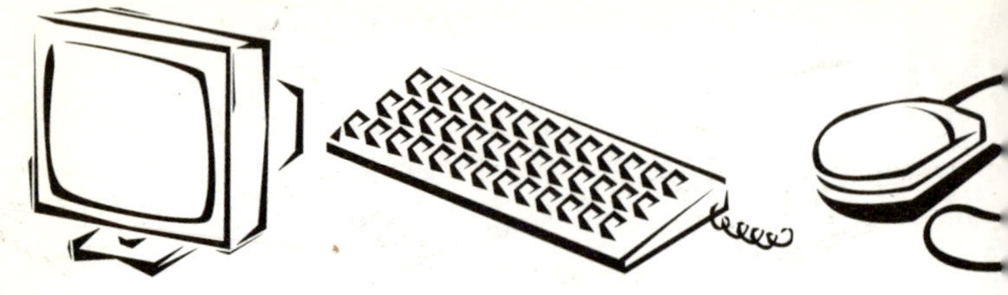

(**www.scooters-uk.co.uk**) receives 30,000 hits a day. Yet Dominic still runs his business entirely off his own bat, and somehow finds time to study for his GCSEs at Forest School in Snaresbrook, London.

Surely he's the most popular guy in school. 'I don't like to say yes. I try to be modest. But quite possibly.' And what about girls? 'Well there's none on the agenda, but I'm sure there's a few that would like to be.' One thing's for sure – he shouldn't have any problems with Business Studies. 'I'm not sure how to approach my teacher any more,' admits Dominic. 'Most of the time he doesn't know what I'm talking about.

'If I didn't have to sleep I would be working on the business twenty-four hours a day, seven days a week. I find it fun. Instead of sitting at home playing games, I get on the phone, meet new people, make new contacts, maintain web sites. I do go out with my friends, but I have to sacrifice a lot. I've got the rest of my life to live. If this is a nice earner, I don't have to worry about the future.'

Right now, all Dominic can think about is his latest

> *'It's quite difficult because you have to learn your balance – don't use the brake first because you might fall over a lot. I fell over once when there were bumps and cracks and things in the pavement. You go in one of those and it flips you. But you can watch people on the street and learn from them, because it's not that hard.'*
>
> *Antonia, 11, Micro*

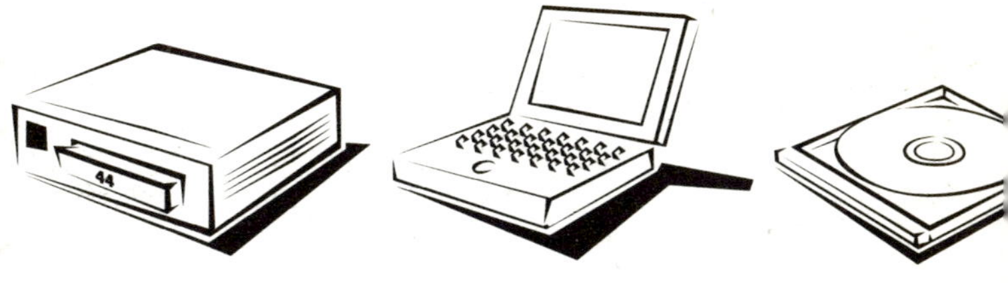

push scooter, the Viza Kikit, which he reckons will outsell the Micro. It's got six-inch pneumatic tyres and mini-spoke wheels, a wider deck for more foot room, a different folding mechanism, LED lights in the wheels ('It looks as if it's got fire coming out the back') and weighs just three and a half kilos.

'Yesterday I went out on it in London and I had kids running up to me, touching it, saying, 'Where did you get that? Look at those wheels, they're amazing.' I was racing someone round town and they're so much faster – with one push they have to do five. One of their dads was even offering me money for it.'

Dominic's also planning to organize a scooting world championship, with the finals to take place in America. He's also got ambitions to be a television presenter and is developing yet more web sites, not at all scooter-related, but he won't reveal any details right now. 'Some people say I'm the next Richard Branson – and that would be nice. I'll be disappointed if it doesn't happen, but it won't be the end of the world.'

> '**Ever since I purchased it I have become the coolest dude in town. It was one of those things I saw in the window and said, "This thing looks damn cool and loads of fun." The next time I went to the shop it was mine, done deal.**'
> *Aaron, 26, Micro*

The **record breaker**

'It will be one of
the hardest things
I've ever done.'

Feeling a bit sore after a little jaunt down the park on your scooter? Spare a thought for twenty-eight-year-old Matt Perry from Burnley. He's setting off to scoot from New York to San Francisco on a Micro – that's a distance of approximately 3,000 miles straight across the middle of America by push power alone. All in the name of charity, of course.

'I'm going to spend pretty much every day on the road and I estimate it'll take about three weeks if I average around fifteen miles an hour,' says Matt, a marketeer for an Internet company. 'I'll be scooting nine hours a day – a full day's work.' Not everyone's idea of a day at the office.

But then Matt's used to it. He already holds the world record for the longest distance covered in twenty-four hours on a push scooter – 161 miles, set on an athletics track in Nelson, Lancashire, beating the previous record of 150 miles held by Nashrita Fuhrmann from New Jersey, USA.

He also travelled from John O'Groats to Lands End on a Veriflex scooter in 1996, again for charity. Matt completed the trip in five weeks in one piece, even if his right trainer didn't. Despite having hardly ever scooted before (he says he had a 'deprived youth'), he was determined to do the trip in a way that had never been attempted.

'*I bought it to get a bit of exercise – it works the upper-thigh muscle – and save money on tube fares at the same time. Watch out for pot holes though. I didn't see that tiny one and went straight over the handlebars!*'

Claire, 20, Micro

'I'd already decided that I was going to do the journey and then just as I was thinking about it, this kid went past me on a push scooter,' he says. 'I just thought, "There's an idea."' After completing the trip, he was hooked. Two years later, he was at it again, shadowing the first leg of the Tour de France, from Dublin to Cork. 'I was the only person on a push scooter among thousands of cyclists. I was scooting through the night, keeping one step ahead, just following the route.'

This time around, he's going to be the star of the show. *The Guinness Book of Records* people have been notified about his American jaunt and he's going to be filmed before setting off by BBC's *Record Breakers*. Plus, on the Micro, he's going to be using a scooter with much smaller wheels than the ones he's ridden in the past.

'It will be a challenge, there's no two ways about it,' says Matt. 'It will be one of the hardest things I've ever done. I've got to battle against all the elements, the extreme weather conditions ... Anything could happen, but I'm still confident I'll do it.'

He's certainly making sure that he's fully prepared, getting up at six in the morning every day of the week except Sunday to do an hour's training – running and a five-mile scoot – before work. Plus in the evenings he practises capoeira, a bizarre, yet beautiful Brazilian martial art that's a cross between fighting and dancing and is great for improving your balance.

But even with all the training in the world, most people still think he's mad to attempt to cross the good ole US of A on a push scooter. 'I do regard myself as quite an eccentric character,' concedes Matt. 'But I think scooters are an ideal way to promote green alternative travel. And they're good fun as well. They're very liberating – you can be a kid on the scooter.'

stuff you'll find in a scootermaniac's rucksack

* City street map

* **Plasters for knee grazes**

* WAP mobile phone (so you can keep up with the news wherever you are)

* **Tony Hawk's Pro Skater 2 PlayStation game**

* Other grown-up toys, such as Palm Pilot, Pokemon GameBoy

* **WD-40 oil**

* Bottle of mineral water and a healthy snack bar (anything nutritious and loaded with energy)

* **Photos of you on your scooter in exotic locations (outside the Taj Mahal, in front of the Pyramids, etc)**

* Sunblock and lip balm (you tan easier in the breeze, you know)

* **Money (for the bus fare in case you can't be bothered to scoot home again)**

The Wheel Story

They don't just grow on trees, you know.

S cooters have travelled a long way since kids used to make their own by nailing a pair of rollerskates to a piece of milk crate way back in the 1930s. They are the latest in a long line of two-wheeled machines that are just as much fun to play with as they are useful for transport – from rollerskates, rollerblades, skateboards, snakeboards, longboards and BMXs to those ridiculous lie-down bikes. But no other machine is going to have a bigger impact on the start of the new millennium.

The first scooter was invented in Germany in 1816, but it wasn't until the 1950s that kids really got into them. Families were moving out of the inner city into bigger houses on the outskirts so there was more space for children to play in. Scooters became a big hit in the suburbs, but these old-fashioned models were nothing like the sleek machines you see today. On these clunky wooden contraptions you wouldn't have dared try a trick – it was hard enough just to go in a straight line.

Over the years the scooter remained popular, but in the late 1980s inline skating and skateboarding became the trendy way to cruise. The scooter all but disappeared. The Scootech or Ninja Scooter, a scooter with BMX brakes, handlebars and wheels twice the size of today's models, made a final attempt to recapture the dying scooter craze in the early nineties, but to no avail.

It wasn't until the summer of 1999, when the first batch of 20,000 Micros went on sale in Japan, and sold out to eager teens within weeks, that the humble scooter got its foot back in the door. Inventor Wim Ouboter says, 'It was perfect because the Japanese like everything that's hi-tech.

'Also the subway system in Japan is pretty crowded, so if you try to take a foldable bicycle on there you'll probably get knocked down because you take up too

much room. But with the Micro there was no problem. That's why it was so successful.' He's not joking – today 75,000 scooters are sold each week in Japan.

Soon Micros had moved across the Pacific and rolled over Australia in the same way as they had Japan. In the streets of Sydney they were everywhere. But when the Micros arrived in Britain last October, they weren't such an instant hit as they had been over the other side of the world. 'It took a while to kick off here because English people are wary of new trends,' explains Ashley Larkman, a manager at Club Blue Room in London.

'I've owned one since Christmas and since then I have convinced at least twelve other kids aged ten to thirteen to buy one. We have made scooter business cards and started a club. My friends and I have got quite good at performing.'
Adam, 11, Micro

However, the Micros were soon picked up by the 'big kids' – twenty- to twenty-five-year-olds – and they began getting noticed on the streets. 'Once they were starting to be seen around a bit, people were like, "Oh, that's cool actually, I don't mind it",' says Ashley. 'Now, every time you turn a corner you see one.'

'I'm a skateboarder really, but it's fun on these things.'
Jamie, 24, Micro

Scooters became such a hit in big cities like London partly because they were used by adults who saw them as ideal for commuting to work; a way of avoiding rush-hour traffic. But also because the first people to ride and sell them were so cool, the scooter became a fashion statement.

Since London is seen as one of the style capitals of the world, before long everyone else wanted a piece of the action. 'We had people coming in from everywhere round the globe, saying, "We've never seen these

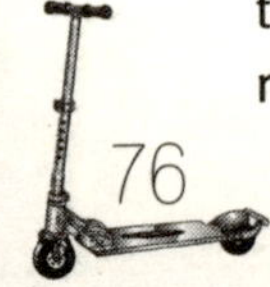

before, these are incredible",' says Ashley. 'Americans loved them. But the biggest fans were the North Europeans – they'd come in and take five back for their kids.'

The Micro is now the highest-selling item in many sports and toy shops, including the world-famous Hamleys in London. Most shops report that they are selling out of scooters as fast as they can stock them. But you won't only find them in specialist stores – you can now pick up scooters in most major high street shops. In the UK they're scooting off the shelves at a rate of around 15,000 a week.

Across the Atlantic, world domination continued when the Micros first arrived in the US after being trialled in the most trend-obsessed state of them all, Hawaii, where their arrival signalled 'mob scenes' in February 2000. They then migrated to the west coast of America and again proved a success with skate dudes and businessmen alike.

But the west coast surfer kids in particular already had their hands full with their very own type of scooter, the petrol-powered Go-Ped. As far back as 1985, Go-Ped founder and inventor Steve Patmont formed family business Patmont Motor Werks in California, to develop and produce his motorized machines. By 1989, he was doing so well that he had to move out of his garage factory. Two years later Go-Peds caught on in the extreme sports world and kids started to race them.

In the mid-nineties, Steve invented Go-Ped's first

non-motorized model, the Know-Ped, and, fuelled by the buzz surrounding the Micro, demand for all types of Go-Ped started to shoot off the skate ramp. 'Our sales have doubled over the year before,' says Steve. 'We can't meet demand.'

At San Francisco gadget emporium Sharper Image, the first store to sell the scooters in the US, the Micro broke records in three months to become the best-selling item the company had. 'It's the hottest product we have ever seen,' says marketing chief Tony Farrell. 'It's the skateboard for people who can't skateboard.'

This new 'skateboard' has now become the top-selling sporting goods product in America, and the scooter love affair is heading north into Canada. Meanwhile in Europe, Micros are selling well in Switzerland, Germany, Austria, Italy, Spain and France. It seems the whole world is going doolally with two-wheeled craziness.

Scootermania has gone truly global.

> **'At first I felt very silly but now I try to concentrate on avoiding potholes. You can go at quite a lick when you've got a clear way downhill.'**
> *Guy, 35, Micro*

> **'You don't have to sit down and take them off like with rollerblades. It really is practical.'**
> *Yilmaz, 23, Micro*

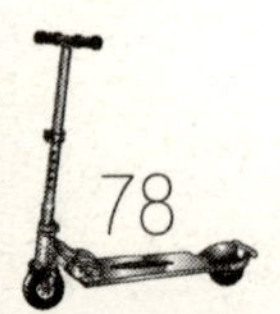

DID YOU KNOW...?

- German MPs use Micros to save time getting around their huge new parliament building.

- The most famous scooter film is called *Return of the Pedi* – a half hour joyride of Go-Ped stunts set to a cool soundtrack.

- Fashion designer Alexander McQueen came out to cheering crowds on a Kickboard after the end of his London Fashion Week show.

- The Micro is known as the Razor outside Europe.

- The French call the push scooter *trotinette*, from *trottoir* (pavement).

- There is a band called Scooter. They're a hard house trio from Hamburg in Germany.

✻ The world speed record on a Micro is
110 km/hour (downhill), set by Juerg
Zackmann in August 2000. The forty-
year-old stuntman and hairdresser
was later stopped by the police
trying to break his own record.

**✻ Offical timekeepers at the Sydney
Olympics were issued with
Kickboards so that they got to
their races in plenty of time.**

✻ In Japan, over 1.2 million scooters
have been sold already.

**✻ One posh customer in London
bought a Micro for pottering
around his huge mansion.**

✻ US supermarket giant Wal-Mart has
ordered three million Micros to sell in
its chain of stores.

**✻ There's a scooter family that
hangs out on Brighton seafront –
the husband, wife and two kids all
have specially customized
machines.**

✻ Using a scooter you burn up at least
300 calories an hour – the equivalent
of a Mars bar.

**✻ A seventy-year-old Dutch lady
bought a Micro on holiday in
London in order to keep up with
her scooting grandkids.**

To Infinity and beyond

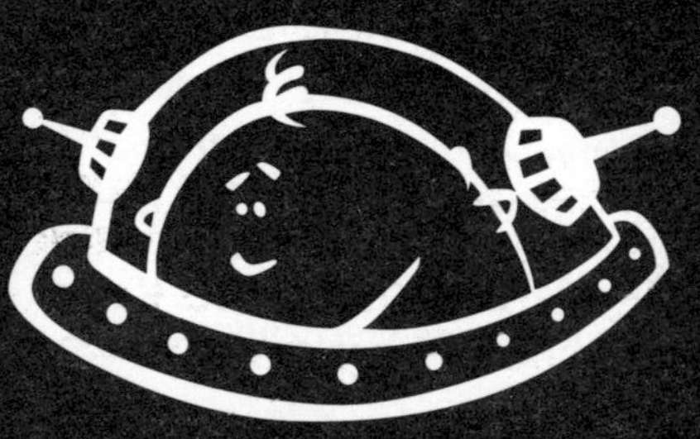

NEW MODELS

The two new models from the Micro stable are the Air and the Airflex. Both have all the features of the Micro Pro, such as front suspension, a wheelie bar and rear LED flashing lights, but the Air has larger pneumatic tyres for a smoother ride, while the Airflex has, surprise surprise, a flexy board too. Further down the line, inventor Wim Ouboter's got something a little bit special up his sleeve. 'We're developing an ABS brake system [used in cars] and a tiny electric engine. The idea is that you push up to five kilometres an hour and then the engine kicks in automatically. It's not for uphill, it's just a really light scooter because it still has to be portable. Our goal is that it should not weigh more than seven kilos.'

> **'I bought one last week in Sydney and brought it home for my children here in South Africa. Brilliant.'**
> *Steve, 36, Micro*

K2 has also just brought out four new types of Kickboard:

* The Kick Two, which has a more sophisticated steering system.
* The Cross Kick, an offroad beast with larger, pneumatic tyres.
* The Absolute Kick with fast slick tyres and a super-wide back wheel for better grip at high speeds.
* The Carveboard, the ace in the pack, a four-wheeled beauty (the two wheels at the front are the larger this time) with a sloping board and a super-sensitive turning mechanism that kicks in at the slightest tilt.

Best of all, prices have come down to street level too.

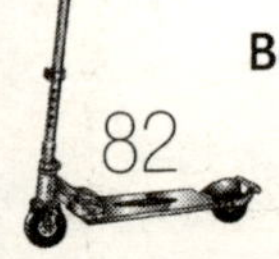

Our tip: You can already buy longboards with built-in electric panels that display start and stop times, date, speed and the distance you've travelled. Surely it's only a matter of time before similar devices start appearing on scooter handlebars.

'I use it to keep up with Dad. He walks too fast.'
Samantha, 9, Micro

INTO THE FUTURE

With a whole supermarket trolley of new machines coming on the market, scootermania shows no signs of slowing down. 'Snowboarding and rollerblading were supposed to be fads too,' says Joseph De La Jara, vice-president of marketing at DLJ International, one of the two major US distributors for the Micro. 'Today, they are still multi-million-dollar businesses.'

'I ride them to school. It's much easier than walking. I can go very fast, but you have to change feet 'cos the foot you stand on gets tired easily.'
Sam, 10, Micro

Skateboards have been around for over thirty years now, so it looks like it shouldn't be too bumpy a ride for scooters, especially with those new pneumatic tyres. Owning a scooter is like owning a bike – once you've bought one, it's always going to be part of your life. And with governments promising to build an ever-extensive network of cycle lanes, scooting is only going to get easier.

The scooter craze will get another push in the right direction as it becomes recognized as an international sport in the same way as skateboarding. The first

scooting World Championships has already taken place in Zurich, Switzerland in September 2000, with speed, slalom and freestyle events, sponsored by multinational companies such as Ericsson and Swatch. Competitions are also planned in England, Germany and France.

Meanwhile, downhill Kickboard racing is a serious sport in Holland. Contestants use special slick tyres and collapse the steering column, crouching down to avoid wind resistance. The Dutch Autoped Federation has been organizing its own races since as far back as 1986, mainly for Kickbikes, but more recently for any form of foot-powered vehicle.

At the same time, scooters are going to become even more accessible to the general public. During the Olympics, scooter rental stations were installed around Sydney, where footsore spectators could hire out a machine for a small fee, returning it to their closest station at the end of the day.

A similar scheme has already been implemented in Berlin. Plans are also afoot to really take advantage of those super-smooth floors and introduce scooters to airports for that last-minute dash to the departure gate. And surely it can only be a matter of time before Sony brings out a scooting game for the PlayStation.

So what's going to be the next craze? Proper hovering boards? Jet-propelled backpacks? Motorized

> *'I received mine as a gift four weeks ago. I took my two kids to ride them down the beach. I was stopped twenty-one times and asked where I got them from and how much they cost.'*
> **John, 37, Micro**

> *'You can really hot dog on this thing. Plus, I feel safe because one foot is on the ground, which is the important thing.'*
> **Kaarin, 22, Kickbike**

trainers? Who knows? But the latest fad to come out of the US is something you couldn't even make up – dog scooting. It's the ultimate slacker's method for exercising your furry friend – forget pushing, you just stand on the scooter while Fido pulls you along.

'To dog scooter you need a dog who likes to run, a harness, a tug line and a scooter,' says Daphne Lewis. 'Scooting after a running dog is more fun than walking with a dog on a leash.' If you don't believe us, read her book, *My Dog Likes to Run, I Like to Ride*.

Are you a scooter maniac?

Do you know your Bunny Hops from your Bonuses? Your Ollies from your Wheelies? Try this fun quiz to find out whether you're a genius or a dunce at the School of Scooter Skills.

1. After your very first go on a scooter you could just about manage:

a. a couple of Tail Whips and a One-Foot Air – no worries.

b. after hours of practice, an Ollie to be proud of.

c. to get off the scooter without bashing your shins with the board.

2. You can tell your scooter from everyone else's because:

a. it's got stunt pegs on the front wheels and your name stuck on the board in reflective vinyl lettering.

b. it's super shiny, well-oiled and given lots of tender loving care.

c. erm, I'm just trying to remember where I left it.

3. You hit a hole and fly off your scooter in front of everyone. Do you:

a. do a quick backflip to land back on your machine, moving swiftly into a dramatic 180-degree Revert. Hey, it's a trick no one's ever seen before (and aren't ever likely to again)?

b. pretend you're limbering up for a Crouch – always best to practise on dry land, you know?

c. scoot off as fast as your one little leg will take you?

4. At night you toss and turn, dreaming about being:

a. the boss of a top international scooter company.

b. the owner of a brand new Carveboard.

c. wrapped up in cotton wool.

5. A 'Cherry Picker' is:

a. easy-peasy.

b. tricky, but you're getting there.

c. someone who sells fruit for a living.

6. When you're out scooting, other people usually:

a. gather round you, clapping and whooping at your incredible array of stunts.

b. don't take much notice (unless you bump into them, silly).

c. point at you and fall over laughing.

7. Before the scooter craze happened, you:

a. were a complete skateboard freak.

b. sometimes went rollerblading.

c. lounged around on the sofa in front of the telly (nothing much has changed then).

8. Finish the following sentence. 'I need my scooter because ...'

a. my life wouldn't be complete without it.

b. it's the most fun you can have on two wheels.

c. my bike got stolen last year.

Turn over to see how you scored!

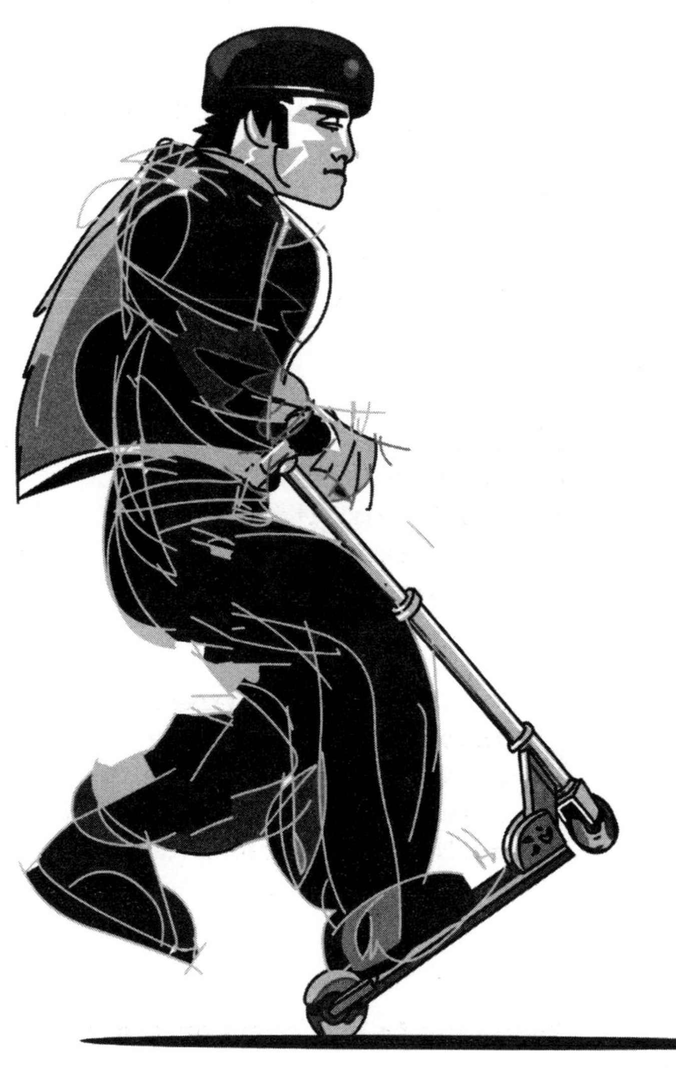

89

Report Card

Count up your score to see how many As, Bs or Cs you got.

Mostly As

You are one *serious* Scootermaniac. Cool and collected, especially when under pressure, you were able to scoot before you could walk (hey, you only need one leg after all), and you're only truly happy when you're on wheels. In fact, you've already got another couple of subjects under your belt – having got top marks in both skateboarding and rollerblading. There's no doubt that you've swotted up on each and every trick in the book and, let's face it, you're something of a scooting know-it-all. The thing is, you find it all wheelie easy! An asset to any scooting school.

Mostly Bs

As far as scooting goes, you're a solid grade-B student. You're having a wicked time with your new

speciality but don't take it *too* seriously. You've got plenty of potential and can turn it on for exam situations, but you're happy either to leave the super-advanced stuff to the real keenos or to copy their stunts at your desk with your finger skateboard when no one's looking. After all it's not just about learning, but hanging out with your mates and having a bit of a laugh. A little bit more concentration and you should do well in the future.

Mostly Cs

Oh dear. You're really not applying yourself. When it comes to scooting, you're taking one step forwards and two steps backwards. You lack so much motivation we really wonder why you bother turning up with the scooter at all – perhaps your parents are forcing you to make an effort because they've spent so much money on your scooting education. One thing's for sure, you were sitting at the back of the class paying so little attention to what was going on around you that this craze has really got you in a spin. Unless you get some stabilizers, we think it might be better if you stayed at home from now on. You're disrupting the others.

Keep on scooting!